T0363389

## Other titles in the UWAP Poetry series (established 2016)

'Alice Savona is a distinctive voice in contemporary
Australian poetry – drawing upon a postmodern repertoire
whilst remaining grounded in deep-seated human concerns.
The poems are characterised by their strong visual elements,
their droll/ironic wordplay and their awareness of the
dilemmas of auto-biography in this age of pervasive social
media. Alice Savona commands a variety of 'vernaculars',
ethnic, occupational and particularly those of the social
media and popular culture – from Doctor Who to Thom
Yorke's bands Radiohead or Atoms for Peace – though
perhaps mostly the latter, for at times the linguistic activity
has the feel of functioning at an "atomic" level, with its
fragmented syntax, abbreviations, isolated syllables,
re-spellings, omissions, stutterings, which collectively
build a landscape of mild threat. Tellingly, though, it is
often whilst one is occupied with this unique battery of
language/s that there comes a needle-sharp jab of emotion:
exemplifying Roland Barthes' punctum – the wounding,
personally touching detail which establishes a direct
relationship with the object or person described.

'I love the energy that these poems display. I love their
difference. And (to quote Alan Wearne's essential
ingredients for a good poem) their mix of wit, music and
passion. Her work is amongst the best of those young writers
ushering in a dynamic era in Australian poetry.'

**John A. Scott**

# Self ie

**Alice Savona**

Alice Savona is a poet and psychologist living in Macedon Ranges, Victoria. She learned an art of poetry from her teacher Claire Gaskin.

# Alice Savona
## Self ie

Poetry

First published in 2020 by
UWA Publishing
Crawley, Western Australia 6009
www.uwap.uwa.edu.au

UWAP is an imprint of UWA Publishing,
a division of The University of Western Australia.

Copyright © Alice Savona 2020
The moral right of the author has been asserted.
ISBN: 978-1-76080-108-3

 A catalogue record for this
book is available from the
National Library of Australia

Designed by Becky Chilcott, Chil3
Typeset in Lyon Text by Lasertype
Printed by McPherson's Printing Group

 uwapublishing

**in recognition of :**

Woodend, Estoril & Howth

slip skin (b) (d) (l) (r) ust

pat's love in shadows

1991, MAZE & acid

jennifer furphy

claire gaskin

reuben j

remy j

paul

**&**

hin

# Contents

# i.   this, my face, before birth

¿

we fissure & fondant dice
Hineni & candy to maybe
re-order the flesh of feeling
thrice edit cell suck addicts


& | &

# CV

let's play *Survivor* psychology
I sculpt eyelids for your snakes
hang your stress from mother's best tree
bring you back clean as Vietnamese salad

I sculpt eyelids for your snakes
the opiate baby is now thirteen
bring you back clean as Vietnamese salad
elliptical stories of bruises on bread

the opiate baby is now thirteen
*I didn't hit him* mum cries in her spoon
elliptical stories of bruises on bread
chunking his chair at a system's red face

*I didn't hit him* mum cries in her spoon
girl buries dad in a pile of gold glitter
chunking his chair at a system's red face
whoever can hurdle the most shit wins

girl buries dad in a pile of gold glitter
hang your stress from mother's best tree
whoever can hurdle the most shit wins
let's play *Survivor* psychology

# Submission

*Sugar* appealed for its ~~inventiveness~~ dissociative, so was ~~shortlisted~~ snorted, ~~but~~ & I am sorry to say I had to ~~reject~~ accept that ~~poem~~ kick & many others that were ~~attractive~~ deviant because of constraints of ~~page~~ ~~numbers~~ pretty cons; I could make an ~~anthology~~ affirmary of all ~~poems~~ addictions with such appeal, if ~~chance~~ pluck permitted. Please do consider sending ~~other work~~

c
a
n  o  c  e  b  o
d
y


during the next ~~submission~~ ~~period~~ nix.

# Self ie

The sap of his word on a headboard
He comes out of jail a famous poem
All line rush buttons bordering breath
Exquisite: our history of hedges

He comes out of jail a famous poet
Squinting to see if she's carrying commas
Fuckled: our shapeless reunions
Eyes of his whites too close again

Squinting to see if she's cockled the commas
At night: he writes: or details a seam
Eyes of her whites too close again
You don't love people so they'll do what you want

At night: she writes: or details her dream
All lines rush as the drafts draw breath
You don't love people so you'll do what they want
The self ie of his poem

# Sandringham

{     To intro miscellany poetry
{     I shortlist cinnamo seizure
{     our lint & liver of leaving

{     we shortlist cinnamo selfies
{     at first ~~it only matters that we rhyme~~

{     first: our sugar simmer cell suck slow

```
                                    b
                                    e
                                    e
                        m   e   e   p
```

{     our font for fathers fuckled
{     em broi dered in to sub text ¿

| Brother | Father |
|---|---|
| above black denim | two parents in my hair |
| and narcissistic feet | one when frizzy, one when straight |
| a metronome | Asperger's + dandruff |
| | |
| Made In Jamaica | Made in Malta |
| | |
| keyboard weeps | so many books the first floor tires of |
| hymnology, reggae, olive sweat | his post-modern tea party |
| as our baseline sleeps | expired spice |
| | |
| Savona Records | Savona ATM |
| | |
| routine is no muse | the part that loves me is grey |
| serial goddess spread | feather-tipped |
| while I wait in my Sunday best | best semiotics posted |
| she sucks on his filthy toes | |
| | |
| *He's the creative one you know* | *We do seem to be a creative family,* |
| | *that includes you too* |
| | |
| in a dancehall | in a theatre |
| my gig breaks | time breaks |
| a pear tree | academic bestseller props us up |
| mother's watching window | chocolate and French crumbs |
| butter on the earlobes for | |
| our feline chord, Goush | |
| | |
| 3081 friends | 59 female partners |
| | |
| produce engineer songwrite | another designer postcard |
| my dub love refund, | our purchase in language |
| reunion tune | |

# Mother                                        Me

two parents in my fits          I will pick all the sultanas from your cereal
absence, presence                         you will cheat on your lover
almond gaze                                      but blame me for Oedipus
                              as officious women eat me with cream

Made In Korumburra                                Made Exuberant

sewing my silhouette breast              on the slide of my t-zone
she never has foot odour                rosehip feminist crumbs
                                                          mad to write

Savona Clothing & Critique                          Aerosolise

routine is God                            10 gotta getta baggage
my words too rich                         20 gotta getta tickets
while Sunday's wine moves down the line   30 gotta getta baggage
she prays her forever                     40 gotta getta tickets

*Carry my anxiety but don't add to it*

in a womb
instinct breaks                                      but *I* like to argue
ox tongue and lemon rind         chocolate mousse and ovaries
embroidered into subtext                     the caffeine in detail
love without empathy is such a plain cami

$10K per holiday                    30 cents owed on a post-it note

please be moved                                    Kol Hakavod
please open your window for       please bring your best honey
my confirmation                     to drizzle on the mindfucks
my standing o

# Menu

### arrival

flipbook womb

ox tongue & lemon rind

### start

Jupiter static of prong | plate | pry

presence | absence

cold cherry soup

### middle

father raised a stage      mothermute

semiotics      calm harm

a hat-pin, a harem's      atom whipped

font for fools without fathers      passive aggressive Tupperware

a pub-din, a flotsam's      silhouette alarm

### finish

hypothesis →

# Hypothesis

Father (f) (h) (ch) ucks mother

when it is really his own fears & | &

anxious avoidance of recovery

that he needs to (f) (h) (ch) uck;


Mother (f) (h) (ch) ucks father

when it is really her own fears & | &

anxious attachment to discovery

that she needs to (f) (h) (ch) uck.

# Deedee

light aunt

    testy sherry

                    tripe & trifle

                sarcastical put

            temple / tension / sap to soot

            cinnamon secret      tappling root

uncled on pheromone   oestrogen loot

          tri ples / trifles / lilies ?put

             template : tension v (s) (r) (l) oot

            dewy   x   surcharge

                    pirouette-mute;

       pack gang 11       hills hoist moot

   rumsreasonsaims

                !serotone woot

          tripe & trifle      neatly shoot.

# It's Quiet in Cuenca

yellow metal traces threads
tapas    churches    antique memory
until we arrive at the beautiful door:
*They don't eat here until 10pm*

i trip cherry flare sangria short soup
i silted    squash seizure
but he, who is he, of Asperger's & dandruff,
will not hold

my hand back to the beautiful door:

*People might think we are a couple*

my father, oedipal punch
guava + chocolate
mosaics cracking
inch by ink to Madrid.

# Adjectives

**Progress Report for:** *Arminel*

**Grade:** *1B, June 1979*

**Physical Education:** *Enjoys all forms of physical activity*

**Music:** *Arminel is enthusiastic & cooperative*

**Oral Language:** *Speaks clearly & fluently*

**Written Language:** *She's able to write very interesting sweet spook wrists*

**Reading:** *Excellent*

**Word Study:** *Puce | brass | headlong*

**Handwriting:** *Very tidy & letters well formed*

**Cultural Subjects:** *Contributes a great deal*

**Mathematics:** *Handles mathematics very well*

**General Comments:** *Arminel has a bright personality & is a ray of sunshine during discussions or group activities. Her enthusiasm never wanes which is inspiring for a teacher.*

# Nouns

1am window
light student jumps
dew | tulle | bee semen

# Verbs

her milk blink
your buggy black

rock | pawn | cell count

I wait light
mother's best pearls

suede & silver knock up the night

only she, at perigee
gets herself see-through
in your last sky

slip skin dust
as I rotate,
her CV eclipses
our saturate sun.

---

**CV**: Critical Voice: imposed w/in systems to: fuck w/ before-birth faces

# Part of Speech : CV

Camden: bootleg bless

        Barbican: Mapplethorpe fists

                Womb: eyelash ellipsis

    1972 ↔ auto

    intergen | chamois | matriarchs

    axe ax infant omphalos

    sewing our silhouette nests

    *Why won't you flesh her to chocolate?*

    *Don't you love her?*

    Blow off a silhouette breast

    high I cassonade burial

    caramel | cognitive | capital

    ← 2020 | self ie →

---

**CV:** I ghost-gaffed filter for incoming silver:

        *There is such so wrong with*
        *every me ¡*

## ii.    de facto, no priors

# First Date

Vodka purrs to tune a Tardis     :     { IN UTERO
{ IVY AND THE BIG APPLES
{ LOVELY CREATURES
{ SUMMER TEETH

{ CALIFORNICATION
{ MASTER OF PUPPETS
{ OK COMPUTER

{ CHAOS A.D.
{ GET BEHIND ME SATAN

{ NEVERMIND

# Conscious.

Me, A. (1972) *Cell Suck*

Father: French crumbs in aerograms

Mother: real v. ideal abandonment

Womb: my face before birth

He, B. (1973) *Flotsam*

Father: inside blue free

Mother: pinkcamipushprettythroat

Womb: a hat-pin, a pub-din

# Un-conscious.

I draft miscellany honey         { Mother (1942) *Sweet Spook Wrist*
his eyelids for my snakes         { Father (1943) *Aspycottonpurr*
our moot for dew wins funding
love in a key of tricyclics

my fyrhto his sherbet fondle
his lint & my liver of leaving
love as a silhouette Sexton
shifting props of swan light

my lint & his liver of ducking
our slomo tulle of true
sifting pheromone memory
shiver_huddle_porcupine_prickle

our slomo grasp of change
moots for margin spill funding     ;
push-pull-porcupine-cycles     .
Miscellany marriage        b
                              e
                              e
             m   e   e   p

Their dolorous keys,

closing my synagogue,
I inchoate.

A kiss with a fit for entrée.

For manyprettyfortypushed but never river through to
what men said: James Bay between, bergamot quills, Chris' coin
from grandmother –

when my Granny died – cammied – camembered  –  she said
*Poor little Arminel, your terrible life!*                                   but
that wasn't life    it was oars    of trying                    hours
of lyings & whatever men bled                                    erect
to bait, Bennelong, when Byron had rabbit.

When my Granny lived she froze

forty-five vegemite sandwiches before sailing to China,
curled caramels as I slept off acid
under the Christmas table, prettier bent & as
men fed, she brandied the best expression of interest
                                        one who murmured
*I'm not sure it ever really happened* that afternoon when I was five & cartilaged
velour dints, becoming what men dread.

Commandeering porcelain: *At least you've got a pretty face.*

Props, of swan light.

When my Granny passed through us – acerbed – cell sucked –
my cob dreaming her anise air,
our male embryo led, she said: ~~aambi~~ ~~ampersand~~ ~~corset~~ ~~dothep~~

*This, my face, before cinnamon chilblains.*

**Swept.**

## IQ

coding

similarities

block design

embroiled

exquisite

boiled

enchanted  bed  wet  x  ray

*There are interactional stressors to consider.*

## EQ

sensory

sensitive

lemongrass

expert

botching

memory

one remarkable boy

made of Lego and honey

posted in public areas

## P&Q
how headbands smell

                              } *Kindly print or fwd.*

    hobbling doors

little metal attachment on spin
delicate period of parental ambivalence


## FU
*Indicative Self ie.*

grief of graffiti ambling
hung up in your notebook

kindly close me
+ milk until menopause

# Milk

after 'Poem' by Simon Armitage

And if in trifle thumos lilied ?pride
he read a vodka tossing history.
And always dewy closed his heart to see.
And slippered slips my postage now for free.

And wifri egg snag egress pathos tripe.
And if he's angry no (3)(2)(1) hide.
Andifinbutter    rum clink of he } me.
Mootsbytownpsych$2.10    per } tweet.

And if in stains & thumos | fuss collide.
And I my knees to detail kitchen stiles.
And sip (1)(2)(3) (k)(n)(r) ip up thighs.
And twice he tri ples love my self ie.

Here's how we rate the milk when we look back;
Sometimes he moos light, sometimes I lap cracks.

# Bread

Hipster holds his axe
delusions of   flux   thaw   yolk

I Ruby Rose residual
the pink tic in his gmail

coo-ees something skewed
for self-defence in            fugues.

The fleece lap | to meconium head | so
the molesters find us sugar,

milk inside *The Lifted Brow*
for anything by Irvine, anything well

before pussies re-shaped themselves as diamond rings
letting shine tilt it breaks.

Babies in bread. A child frying denim in anise & venom
for the adult re-homing her hedge,

as he reads a vodka
& hopes in line;

# Sugar

tripe or trifle
sweet daisy snow
pink tic memory
fleece lapped foe
drink until friendly

silhouette blow

pillowy          vain
snuff  smut  mane

drink until friendly


sweet daisy snow

anise on venom
drink until friendly
g-mailed toe

rum in my row
snuff  smut  blow

coupon kaleidoscope

every sun of blanket gun
his face wifri foe


white out beers
narcissistic toe

duck_l_ing throat
pink tic twitter

self ie stain
collapse under train
moots by town psych
tripe & trifle

stuck at our vein

cell suck slow

# Head –

tik tak

butterfly vat

; the eyes of your whites too close again


**honchoed** slip in self


your bullock neckline

drunk on our corridors {


eat me officious & right me with cream

**but**

donotpresssendinthis

          6 months, of interrelated skirts + smiles

          at night : I write : or detail the bannisters

          looking forward to liverwurst

          **jobs**


          then you switch to the soul of a Datsun

          blossy    blind    cc'd

          scent **of our OCD**, see

  embroiled

Insomnia April 12 tries                    y              unfortunate fiancé

    poem after swagger                     e              staying in the city

corset carves pink fry                     r

arse: fistula tarantula                    v                    To revive

arcade insomnia April                          o                    keep

    12 tries poem after                    y

# Bathrings

boiled   exquisite                April 12 tries poem

forgets to      ,      s          after swagger acid

for one more drink.    e          borderline ask:

                                  fistula tarantula arcade insomnia

                    l             always the danger of 1, 2, 3

ink,                 f            buttons bordering breath

writing:              i           Ileana 80s Maltese death

                   e              my will to wash

                                  all of your human

                                  precious

                                  swagger other posts

                                  her husband's hat: fistula

                                  tarantula arcade insomnia,


they're affairs because they're   **secret**.

# Vanity

# Gravity

*Skinn* by Dimitri James
TVSN falls on my wagon
dope  adulterate  deaden  soak

*The Checkout*
ABC by Aunty Neroli
your mother's chin is not
commodity

*@ 35 the dermal junction breaks!*

*You're right, Dim, it is @ 35,*
*almost overnight my chin*
*just dropped!*

*Stem-regen-serum*
*tap, tap, tap*
*don't be afraid to tap!*
*Look at that difference!*

exquisite: our history of bunions
as I stare at nasturtiums
& public drovers

*Gosh!*

*I can make it look better*
*if I tap more...*

*Girls: are you the 'Firm & Lift' –*
*do you have a double chin –*
*or are you 'Redensifying'*
*your old chooky neck?*

I'll tap your horror show
I'll $59.50
your psychotic dermi
won't fuck with my get

age on grace
co-sleeping cash
coupon   kaleidoscope
innocent breath s

# Verisimilitude

After our first session we (f) (h) (ch) ucked five times
embroiled | boiled | exquisite
sueded red downstairs. Mulled wine's fine a.m. Muted
for the second session: *Lists don't work for him.* Thick calm
for a side of things, bulk of a counsellor counting hymens.

Contain: *your anger & anxiety in private or express in an adult way
that is not dismissive.*

But there wasn't any wind that day, so the list I'd compiled in b/w
sex sat hell
one orgasm away from suede, evidence tipsy on slander.

The brutal bulk drank dollar longings; ate burnt caramel words
to start us
again in oral haze. Cherry-flared theory sliming his tongue:

*You are around kids all day & are slipping into crying
as a way to get what you want.*

## splitSpilt

bottom lip drip, drake
detour our expensive, unfair, fair therapist with huge feet & excellent
eye contact on tap.    My call    my fault    s  s  slow like lavender  : -
as I high cried the hypno brutal bulk stuck his tongue out further:

*He finds your tears more alien than your anger.*

Dream shit is odourless.
Androphobia is fear of men.
The list was literal. But what it really said, was:

    there) my petticoat-pink revolution
    here)  your dust, on laminate sex
    b/w)  bolognese lies & ablution & gabardine kiss & dead clean rush.

At our third session, the hulk of a hypno brutal bulk ended:
*You are up here & he is down there*         *on the red suede,*
as cool as my drake, both with their flat rates & composure.

HHHBB, at the edge of mohair, one eyebrow for the straight people.

# Scaffold

1. Prodrome: our conscious flotsam

2. Pheromone feast of: trauma

3. Coupling + light + cracks = sugar

4. Domestic deposition: red

5. Dance: do I need to break up w/ hipster or w/ my own funk projected on to him?

# Reference

Eyelids for your snakes

!serotone woot

Love sapping sous

!serotone woot

The I of our Tardis

!serotone woot

Sexton's row | s    neatly shoot.

# Prognosis

*Our good days & bad days & fuss* mutters God
our hiccup of peace | bit of this | spit of odd

## IQ2

afternoon detox
green toilet full
of mint

## Blood TARDIS

he can't name feelings

          invisipl spill

Tom Baker's two hearts fly towards calves

         i've got a thing

o, i, y

        you_don't_love_people_so_you'll
        do_what_they_want

stuck.

        at adrenarche

Daleks on a bus

        lint notes

over-bite

        blackforest fuss

blossy –

        blind cc'd

Thom Yorke's beat brain

        adored  alone  ordered  alone

inside blue free

        : just do what works

our folio of bruises

        be you on Gallifrey

and I'll be the owl;

# M | e

I can't name nixes
                              I whypipe faith
Tom Baker's two hearts fly towards scars
                              his yeah | nah | yeah
                    her pink tic twitter
                              you don't love people
                              so they'll do
                              what you want.

**iii.**
**puspinkcamipushprettymythroat,**
**poet + petticoat =**

# Illumin | e

We progress, our folio of bruises
ease hypothetical T&Cs –

@ our next ketamo ¡ sex I text :

r
e
t i m e .
r
o

## as is I is as

; so sweet my anxious addiction. To his avoidant attachment.
To the fonts of my inner critic & its overeaten, bloody bio.
I am puce, brass, headlong. He is tulle, dew, bee semen.
The psychologist strikes: *Contain your identity-anxiety in private,
or express in a non-dismissive way.*
Now we are quiet, our shadow a Tardis.
The clocks drip caramel. Cotton finds fuse blues for Gallifrey.
We notate heavy dismissals; flipbook fear of self.
A mercy simmer cell suck slow.

presence                                         absence
lineage & peaches                           lineage & pus
tadpole hours                                  tadpole years
Hineni, honey                                        acoria
                                                    acid tic teapot
                                                    caffeine detail
alkaline linen                          a hat-pin, a harem's
                                                    acerbic clout
sift doubt & pour                      filter | wild | whip
                                                    curds of agreement
rubella piggy backs                          olympic tears
amphetamine silk                          ampersand milk
                                    purrs
                                    fits
                            porcupines

creativity takes courage        sterile imaginative self ie
            | matisse |                              | me |

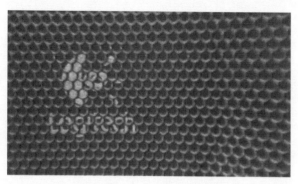

Her kerosene closh c　l　o　s　e　s

my why pipe | iscellany | meta me

Jupiter Static of borderline slur:

*My kid said your kid keeps calling him 'fag' & he's asked him to stop but*
*he won't.*

The anxious attachment of cinnamon Jung s

mythink | herthink of o t h e r  m o t h e r s

; clean to the coccyx

| our antimony arsehole s

antifantasy raisin moss

cornflowered candy helicopter s

I, neroli nigh her my write

right one less nix into overbite.

Fusing a fig leaf for Facebook s

triple | bind s | baled

my self ie closh o p e  n  s | @ butterfly justice | slabbed off instinct:

## A Chardonnay Bully is Harder to Prove

# NET

| The Crown | Love |
|---|---|
| Camden Queen | our opine hope in elegant walls |
| Sandringham Queen | silver slick tics     poesis of trauma |
| Coupling Queen | our wildly different work of self ie |
| Cisgender Queen | our lips bunting for bathrings, for |
| Selfie Queen | what else can we do to ~~hypocrisy~~ ᶜ |

31:20 ⎯⎯⎯⎯⎯⎯⎯⎯⎯⎯⎯⎯⎯⎯⎯⎯⎯⎯⎯⎯⎯⎯⎯⎯⎯⎯⎯⎯⎯⎯⎯⎯

# FLIX

| The Alienists | Me |
|---|---|
| I learn more from Netflix than | love in a key of tricyclics, I |
| anything presence v absence | anxious attachment to self ie |
| corked; it ~~tells~~ shows how our | pheromone memory fits |
| cassonade alienation | cinnamo comatose debtors |
| before-birth faces are directed ¡ | drinking me eyeless @ $13.99 |

_____ 09:37

# HowToBeHappyWhenYou'reDead

**1.**

record taboo

tinny bloom

into eviscerate after                    | life like sequential flowering


**flip.**

plummy grid      hock & slid

litmus } cinnamon { pimp


**3.**

an angel reverses

your public soul                    | like life-heist

sift prudence & pour

**for.**

God will fry a blue, true sentence

sex:  nox  gore  orgid

ghost gaffing golden blocks


**barter.**

your carni flutter                    |  lifelike bootleg

dim after noir

our villanelle harbour.

# Alexithymia

synonym : pheromone : tic
my folio, his bruises
embroidered into subtext
sex the ¡ of extraordinary


my omphalos, his ox tongue
dismiss | avoid | discovery
change the ¡ of relapse
love, a silhouette breast

attach | detach | recovery
how he hangs his thoughts
love, a silhouette Sexton
ire, flesh of feeling


how I hang my thoughts
embroider picket nests
settle flesh of self ie
synonym : marriage : repeat :

# FEMIN

Mymanyprettyfortypush
Our sons damn s burst at coz.am ; even the coat hangers.
I look under publisher for suburb s
We will wander. One more drink & dangle.
They want to wash bones  { wipe away whiz. *Now that we're*
opt to know less ; beetled, beautymythed ; tinderbox whipbird.

*I'm going to marry my paintings!* | *My iPad password is 'I love Mama!'*
*carbon patois grit?* | *Why* *when*
*we could heist it?*

*cuddling our shadow is a love heart.* The way we get out of cars *hope*
Puspinkcamipushprettymythroat *for* ?poet + penis =

# FRAZ

Hipster: hem: forty s. Dub: your tea-towel s
through our bitten door. On dope rack s sit your choice s:

i.        *keep cinnamon tea-cake warm*

ii.       *choke other till cold.*

Sift resistance & pour, button s bordering breath s ;
your father's flipbook hand smoking solution.

Up Yeats' hill in Howth

delicate crepe w/ blackout
or
bitten door thaw to iii. vodka fold.
Biscotti spit recovery
our reed | read s protecting hope

as


you opt to know more, lift cumin & cool, love's silhouette sous –

# The Way We Get Out Of Cars

A
time poor fret plays 6, 5, 4
hypotenuse skid  /  cinnamon door
bang in key his peperine stare
buttercup cross-cut #lair

hummus heart looking for:  cinnamon █
her two tic rule  }  for crying on the floor
blue tits & Abagail  >  mouth full of hair
shipwreck squash  v  pluck corsair

♊ second rule  }  for crying on the floor
03 – limb – 7 – love – 1 – claw
forfeit mosh  |  coked au pair
easier to litmus lie than execute care

03 – limb – 7 – love – 1 – bawd
bang in key his flipbook fare

🚌  🚌  🚌  🚌  🚌  🚌  🚌

her borderline tap drips 6, 5,
4.

# Tree Change

## Monday

An 80s flair for cell suck.

Years to yolk it | slab it | felt it.

*Yes-yes,* seeps the editor, *more poems bout FathersMothersSistersBrothers*
but buddy, who else hucked the volume? Humble ankles, yellow knees.
Pleading with my matriarch for 3 Weet-Bix a day. So say 2 *Our Father*
*who* & fumble 1 welcome before I reverse, highballed by love.

Legot.

Head on to adrenarche: mental health will be priced on application. By
a red-breast postwoman, parked thrice on your corner, her Campari
tongue not yet set to *melt.*

## Tuesday

You borderline jag hand | drip pink as mother goes to dance | as her mother rips up our poetry.

I loft-lip pride but imposition inks my tell.

I sell death of neighbourhood; hooded neighbours say *all s o r t s of things.*

Bar emotional intuit.

So where was it stamped, your bellissimo right? To parody, chardonnay, sense cinerarium? Subscription to snakeskin & eyelash on ice. Whisper of purses & pristine civics. To fig-leaf Facebook & Tim Winton's sky.

Bay-side.

## Wednesday

*That's absolutely no issue for me* says a crab-apple blossom en route to trapeze. Another man taking his anima for a walk. A Woodend kookaburra regional gig. Fishbowl Coles: balaclava or chat.

& I & my *why* wait at Holgates pub, for lamb slower than cells back to Sandringham.

*You were right.* I trust to tighten hipster's split from the sea.

It ticks all the boxes | I didn't look back.

The photosynthesis of kin.

1 fray, without fire-plan.

## Thursday

But I gag *I'm leaving!* Until he did. Then I set *I'm feeling!* My history grid.

To revive ink: keep writing:

presence | absence | cold cherry soup.

No peace in laps of pickled heed. No fatherly vigour regret. No cells spinning back to *Yes, I can make this right.* All the clock we prickle parenting's reverse veins & jag hands & hooky priors, subject to crumbs & fleece, waiting for the [continuity of] post.

Ball-high love.

## Friday

So I build ?poem for those who built me | *FathersMothersSistersBrothers.*
A sherbet host chasing IQ through pinecones. Omphalos bathed in
saffron; hipster's secrets for tree-change.

Our sequential flowering:

eagle-impaled divorce
pink tic twitter
his g-mailed toe
something 'bout *better be happy than right.*

**Saturday**

The 2am of another town meeting. I'd better go. Am feeling quite creative!

# Sunday

# Claire Gaskin

*Adj* **aerial** | **expert**    *Verb* **poein** | **pseudic**

Her biddy pink   beginner bud s   sit salt class

begin a cinnamo sash

for soft tissue trauma & Sexton's rough ing row s

declension of deed on Trump's tweet tongue

& *all the blue rushing through*

*the pinpoint of an iris.*

Her field to vase course in p ( _____ )     ¿ oesia   oesie   oesis

Monroe toes tap

*two coffees awake on a sea of dead horses*;

our (paper) (pen) (fissures) (rudimentary empathy)

& subop poet pop Popeye submittals.

# Arminel Seizure

*Noun* **flume** | **exuberance**    *Adverb* **fixed ¿**

Her collapse of all gangrenous thesis:

*The closed door is sucked towards the open door.*

Silver sick tics tear

our Tardis to word fare

& Road Runner's serotone woots;

dangled seams of analysis

dry bite flight from submission.

Fang to foot my resistance

to smoke her aniseed ash

her feminist hash, as

*I story my hands to the wall,* she tells me things to last line float.

## Post

Camden: flyers for fox scats    Barbican: Mapplethorpe fists
Womb: 40¢ fonts

Contain: our alexithymic shit

(Mailbag: alkaline linen & amphetamine silk)

*Why won't you flesh me to chocolate?*

& huckle . our . volume's . over - eaten . **Bio**

# Submit

**Active  Accepted  Declined  Withdrawn**

anxious attachment to SteakKnife | SynthPop

**One white poet evokes familiar**

why pipe poet binges relapse

**We do hope you contemplate submitting again**

addtobag | **Add to bag**

anxious attachment Accepted | Rejected

sap **white poet evokes familiar**

why pipe bingers poem relapse

**We can't place your** curtsy **on this occasion**

anxious attachment as YesSuite | NoSuite

sap womb **poet** G-suites **familiar**

gatekeepers binging relapse poets

**We pay $$ to** suckle obscurity


& | ᵹ


anxious attachment our HonourableShame

sap womb poet G-suites litmus

gatekeepers binge editorial splinters

submit to our suckle your shelf life!

# Honey

## Hypothesis

Father (f) (h) (ch) ucks mother

when it is really his own fears & | &

anxious avoidance of recovery

that he needs to (f) (h) (ch) uck;


Mother (f) (h) (ch) ucks father

when it is really her own fears & | &

anxious attachment to discovery

that she needs to (f) (h) (ch) uck.


## Materials

Me, A. (1972) *Cell Suck*    He, B. (1973) *Flotsam*


Father: French crumbs in aerograms    Father: inside blue free

Mother: real v. ideal abandonment    Mother: pinkcamipushprettythroat

Womb: my face before birth    Womb: a hat-pin, a pub-din

# Method

### i. I try contemporary poetry

*Sugar* appealed for its ~~inventiveness~~ dissociative, so was ~~shortlisted~~ snorted, ~~but~~ & I am sorry to say I had to ~~reject~~ accept that ~~poem~~ kick & many others that were ~~attractive~~ deviant because of constraints of ~~page numbers~~ pretty cons; I could make an ~~anthology~~ affirmary of all ~~poems~~ addictions with such appeal, if ~~chance~~ pluck permitted. Please do consider sending ~~other work~~

c
a
n o c e b o
d
y


during the next ~~submission period~~ nix.

## ii. We try contemporary coupling

he : me : candy of cheats
my eyelids for his snakes
embroidered into subtext
sex, the ¡ of extraordinary

his omphalos, my ox tongue
the caffeine in our detail
change, the ¡ of relapse
love, a silhouette Sexton

a fig-leaf for our Facebook
how I hang my thoughts
love, a porcupine cycle
to anchor self ie

what I hang my thoughts on
to sew our silhouette nest
his self ie, my poem
synonym : marriage : repeat :

### iii. He tries contemporary vinyl

Vodka purrs to tune a Tardis       :       { IN UTERO
                                               { IVY AND THE BIG APPLES
                                               { LOVELY CREATURES
                                               { SUMMER TEETH

                                               { CALIFORNICATION
                                               { MASTER OF PUPPETS
                                               { OK COMPUTER

                                               { CHAOS A.D.
                                               { GET BEHIND ME SATAN

                                               { NEVERMIND

### iv. We try contemporary therapy

; so sweet my anxious addiction. To his avoidant attachment.
To the fonts of my inner critic & its overeaten, bloody bio.
I am puce, brass, headlong. He is tulle, dew, bee semen.
The psychologist strikes: *Contain your identity-anxiety in private,*
*or express in a non-dismissive way.*
Now we are quiet, our shadow a Tardis.
The clocks drip caramel. Cotton finds fuse blues for Gallifrey.
We notate heavy dismissals; flipbook fear of self.
A mercy simmer cell suck slow.

**Results**

Me, A. (2020→) ~~I love people so they'll do what I want.~~
He, B. (2020→) *You don't have to be perfect for me to love you.*


**Discussion**
We progress, our folio of bruises
ease hypothetical T&Cs –

@ our next ketamo ¡ sex I text :

r
e
t  i  m  e .
r
o

## Conclusion

*Divorce* appealed for its dissociative, so was shortlisted.

However –

I had to reject that poem because of blinkered (f) (h) (ch) ucks

(the intergenerational transmission of pheromone memory).

I will make an anthology of all armour as pluck permits

& | *&*

as we me-he anchors for sugar,

drizzling trust on your ox tongues,

please do consider sending          the why of your honey v. self ie ¿

# Acknowledgements

Versions of many of these poems have appeared in the following journals:

**Contrappasso:**
*Swept.* (an earlier version published, 2015)

**Cordite Poetry Review:**
*CV* (NO THEME II, 2013)
*IQ* (CONSTRAINT, 2014)
*Self ie* (TRANSTASMAN, 2015)
*Honey* (PEACH, 2019)

**Etchings:**
*Brother Father Mother Me* (2013)

**Flash Cove:**
*Sugar* (2016)
*FEMIN* (2016)

**otoliths:**
*Submit* (2018)
*FRAZ* (an earlier version published as Ascent, 2018)
*Reference* (an earlier version published as *The Poem | Piss | Pride: DSM-V*, 2018)
*M | e* (2018)
*Unconscious.* (an earlier version published as *Coupling*, 2018)

**Rabbit Poetry:**
*Vanity Gravity* (Gravity, 2013)
*Verisimilitude* (an earlier version published in Deviations, 2015)
*Bathrings* (Geography, 2016)

**Scum Mag:**
*The Way We Get Out Of Cars* (2016)

**Shots from The Chamber:**
*Tree Change* (an earlier version published in Chamber Poets Anthology, 2016)

**The Hunter Anthology of Contemporary Australian Feminist Poetry:**
*Deedee* (2016)

**The Journal of Post-Colonial Modernist Fiction**:
*Verbs* (an earlier version published as *Last Sky*, 2015)
*It's Quiet In Cuenca* (2015)

~~**UNUSUAL WORK**~~:
*Bread* (2016)
*Milk* (2016)
*Animal Seizure* (an earlier version published as Sunday, 2018)

**WRIT Poetry Review**:
*Blood TARDIS* (2014)
*Head -* (2015)


A selection of these poems were awarded the *Words in Winter Contemporary Poetry Prize* (2015) by John A. Scott.

*Self ie* won Chamber Poets Reader of the Month (2015)